Original title:
Celestial Affection

Copyright © 2025 Swan Charm
All rights reserved.

Author: Aron Pilviste
ISBN HARDBACK: 978-1-80560-175-3
ISBN PAPERBACK: 978-1-80560-640-6

Cosmic Heartstrings

In the vastness of the night,
A whisper on the breeze,
Stars align, hearts take flight,
Lost in cosmic seas.

Nebulas swirl in dance,
Painting dreams on dark skies,
With every fleeting glance,
Love's light never dies.

Galaxies beckon near,
With tales of ancient lore,
Cosmic heartstrings we hear,
Echoing forevermore.

Through the silence we drift,
On orbits made of fate,
In every starry gift,
Our destinies await.

Hold tight to starlit dreams,
As worlds begin to spin,
Together, it all seems,
A journey to begin.

Embrace of the Milky Way

In the arms of the night,
Galaxies gently sway,
Stars are glowing bright,
In the Milky Way.

Dust and light intertwine,
A tapestry of grace,
In this space divine,
Love finds its place.

Orbiting thoughts collide,
Planets in sweet embrace,
With the universe wide,
We find our space.

Each twinkle a soft sigh,
Each comet a soft dream,
Carried across the sky,
In stardust we gleam.

In the void we are whole,
Infinite paths we trace,
In cosmic shadows roll,
The heart finds its pace.

Reflections on Heaven

Beneath the endless blue,
Wonders drift like dreams,
The sky a canvas too,
Where starlight softly beams.

Each sunset brings a tale,
Of hopes and distant lands,
In twilight's gentle veil,
We grasp with open hands.

Clouds whisper secrets high,
Mirroring our thoughts,
In their grace, we fly,
In the beauty sought.

The moon's soft glow entreats,
A love we cannot see,
In this dance, heartbeats,
Set our spirits free.

Reflections bring us peace,
In the stillness we find,
Moments never cease,
As we drift through the mind.

Heartbeats Among the Stars

In silence, we ascend,
Among the gleaming lights,
With every star, we blend,
In the depths of the nights.

Floating on cosmic waves,
Echoes of dreams appear,
In the world that it saves,
We conquer all our fear.

Galactic rhythms pulse,
Like whispers in the dark,
In every thump and waltz,
Love ignites the spark.

Time holds no bounds tonight,
As heartbeats intertwine,
In this celestial flight,
Hearts endlessly align.

Together, we shall roam,
In the universe wide,
Finding our way home,
With each star as our guide.

Love's Astral Journey

In the silence of the night,
Two hearts dance in moonlight,
Whispers soft, like starlit beams,
A journey born from woven dreams.

Through galaxies, they glide and sway,
Finding warmth in the Milky Way,
Each pulse, a rhythm of the soul,
In love's embrace, they become whole.

Nebulas paint a vibrant hue,
As they explore the vast, anew,
Floating on cosmic tides so free,
Together, they shape their destiny.

Constellations spark with life,
Echoing hope, dissolving strife,
In every touch, a spark ignites,
Guided by celestial lights.

In the expanse of unknown skies,
Their love transcends; it never dies,
A boundless map of tender grace,
Two hearts united in endless space.

Celestial Maps of Affection

Beneath the stars, their secrets glow,
Celestial maps that guide them slow,
Each constellation holds a key,
Unlocking love's sweet mystery.

Planets spin in perfect form,
Creating paths that keep them warm,
Orbiting hearts drawn by the light,
A dance of souls, pure and bright.

In space, they trace their vivid paths,
Laughter echoes, all sighs and gasps,
Charting every moment, close,
In this universe, they chose.

Stars collide, their stories blend,
In vast infinity, love won't end,
For every dawn brings forth a sign,
That in this map, their hearts align.

Through gravity's pull, they intertwine,
In love's embrace, their fates define,
Mapping journeys hand in hand,
In the cosmos, they forever stand.

Heart in Orbit

A heart in orbit spins around,
In quiet worlds, their love is found,
Every pulse, a cosmic beat,
In gravity, they softly meet.

With every turn, the stars align,
Creating paths that intertwine,
In endless skies, they find their way,
A love that shines, come what may.

Each glance holds galaxies anew,
In every whisper, dreams come true,
Through open skies, their spirits soar,
A universe worth fighting for.

As comets streak across the night,
Their bond ignites a brilliant light,
Creating tales that time won't fade,
In the shadows, love's cascade.

A heart in orbit, forever bound,
In the dance of love, they are found,
Through the cosmos, they drift and glide,
With each heartbeat, love as their guide.

Hues of the Universe

In colors bright, the night unfolds,
Brushstrokes of love in stories told,
Every shade a new embrace,
Painting dreams in boundless space.

From deep indigos to fiery reds,
Their love ignites, the cosmos spreads,
With splashes of warmth and tender light,
Creating worlds that feel just right.

Nebulas bloom with every sigh,
Each moment a hue that does not lie,
In twilight's kiss, their hearts align,
A palette rich, a love divine.

The universe swirls in vibrant song,
In every note, where they belong,
Dancing through stardust, hand in hand,
In hues that only lovers understand.

As dawn arises, colors blend,
Their love, a masterpiece without end,
Forever painted on the skies,
In the hues of love, their spirits rise.

Celestial Reflections

In twilight's gentle glow, we dream,
Stars twinkling like whispers of hope.
The night sky unveils its theme,
A cosmic canvas, beyond our scope.

Mirrors of light dance above,
Each twinkle a story, a silent roam.
In the silence, we find love,
A universe vast, yet we call it home.

Planets align in a lover's embrace,
With every glance, a spark ignites.
In the night's comfort, we find our place,
Bound by the rhythm of celestial flights.

Galaxies swirl in a cosmic waltz,
Echoes of laughter, timeless and free.
In the expanse, we find no faults,
Just our heartbeats, in perfect harmony.

Amongst the constellations, we weave,
Two souls entwined in the celestial sea.
In reflections of light, we believe,
Together forever, just you and me.

Universe of Intimacy

In the quiet of night, we share our thoughts,
Whispers of dreams float in the air.
An infinite space where love is caught,
A universe built on moments we dare.

Stars above us, secrets untold,
In their glow, we find our way.
Through the darkness, our hands we hold,
Creating a light that will never sway.

Within this vast universe, we thrive,
Cosmic energies drawing us near.
In the depth of silence, we arrive,
Knowing our love will always steer.

Galactic bodies, tender and bright,
In every heartbeat, we're intertwined.
In this cosmic dance, pure delight,
A universe of intimacy we've designed.

Years may pass, yet we remain,
In this swirling mass, we are one.
Love's gravity, an endless chain,
Forever united, under the sun.

Echoes of Cosmic Love

In the chorus of stars, our hearts align,
With each pulse, love's essence grows.
Across the cosmos, a timeless sign,
Whispers of affection in gentle flows.

Through the nebulae, our stories soar,
Each twist and turn, a path we embrace.
In the void, the heart craves more,
Echoes of love, in infinite space.

Shooting stars etch our names in the night,
Trace the paths of our fervent souls.
Reflections of passion, bold yet light,
In the universe, our love unfolds.

With every heartbeat, the cosmos sighs,
A harmony only the heavens know.
In the stillness, as starlight flies,
Our echoes of love forever glow.

From dark matter to light, we transcend,
Two souls, one journey, forever free.
In the tapestry of time, we blend,
Echoes of love, the heart's decree.

Bows of Stardust

With stardust trails, our paths entwine,
Each moment captured in a celestial arc.
In the quiet night's embrace, you are mine,
A dance of light, igniting the dark.

In the glow of twilight, our eyes meet,
Every gaze a promise, soft and true.
In this realm where time feels complete,
We float on dreams, forever anew.

Across vast heavens, our spirits soar,
The universe humming our sacred tune.
Underneath the stars, we explore,
Fleeting shadows beneath the moon.

Each whisper carries the weight of bliss,
A melody played on cosmic strings.
In the warmth of your smile, I find my kiss,
Bows of stardust, eternal flings.

Together, we ignite a distant flame,
Two hearts ablaze in the cosmic night.
In this starlit journey, love's the game,
Bows of stardust, our hearts take flight.

Love's Cosmic Continuum

In the silence of the night,
Stars whisper secrets bright.
Hearts entwined in cosmic dance,
Every glance a timeless chance.

Galaxies spin, endless and vast,
Moments cherished, shadows cast.
Through the void, our spirits soar,
A love that breathes forevermore.

Eclipsed thoughts in twilight's beam,
We wander through a cosmic dream.
Each heartbeat echoes through the light,
In the universe, we take flight.

Gravity pulls us ever near,
Fate aligned, the path is clear.
With each star, our love ignites,
A tapestry of shared delights.

We spin together, side by side,
In this cosmos, where we abide.
With every orbit, every phase,
Our destinies entwined in rays.

Asteroid Affection

Drifting through the quiet space,
Two asteroids, in soft embrace.
Across the black, they find their way,
In the void, their love will stay.

Craters form, a tender mark,
Lighting up the endless dark.
Each collision, gentle chance,
In the cosmos, a sweet romance.

Floating close, they share a dance,
Timeless waltz, a fleeting glance.
Among the rocks, their love ignites,
In the silence, starry nights.

Space debris can't tear apart,
The gravity of each kind heart.
In their orbit, hands entwined,
Love's magnetic pull defined.

Asteroid affection, fierce and bold,
In the heavens, stories told.
Every moment, a chance to feel,
A love like this, forever real.

Gravity of Your Gaze

In your eyes, a universe,
A pull so deep, I can't disperse.
Gravity binding, soul to soul,
Every look makes my heart whole.

With a gaze, you draw me near,
In your sight, I see my sphere.
Constellations fall in line,
In this moment, your love shines.

Sparkling stars begin to play,
In the warmth of your gaze, I sway.
Every blink, a gentle caress,
In your eyes, I find my rest.

Tidal waves of emotion rise,
Captured deep in those wise eyes.
In your stare, the world aligns,
Time suspends; our love defines.

Hold me closer, don't relent,
In your gaze, my heart is sent.
Every moment, like the sun,
In the light of you, we are one.

Nebulous Wishes

In the clouds of dreams we weave,
Nebulous wishes, hearts believe.
Together we'll shape the night,
As constellations take their flight.

Shooting stars streak through the sky,
Whispers of hope, passing by.
Each desire, a gentle spark,
In the darkness, we leave our mark.

Through nebulas, our wishes swirl,
Laced in stardust, love unfurl.
Every breath a wish takes flight,
In the silence, pure delight.

Let the cosmos hear our plea,
In this vast infinity.
Every dreamage, soft and light,
Wrapped in magic, day and night.

In the vastness, we will stand,
Hand in hand, dreams so grand.
Nebulous wishes, forever flow,
In the heart, our love will glow.

Moonlit Devotion

Under the silver night, we glide,
Whispers of dreams, where hearts abide.
Soft shadows dance, in a gentle sway,
Moonlit devotion, guiding our way.

In the quiet glow, secrets unfurl,
Promises linger, in this enchanted whirl.
With every sigh, the stars ignite,
A tapestry woven, in the heart's light.

Time stands still, in this sacred space,
Bathed in the glow, of your loving grace.
Laughter like music, fills the air,
In moonlit devotion, a love to share.

As the world fades, and silence sings,
We are the echoes of eternal springs.
In the night's embrace, nothing feels wrong,
Our souls in harmony, a timeless song.

When dawn approaches, and shadows flee,
Know in my heart, you'll always be.
For beneath the stars, we found our fate,
Moonlit devotion, an endless state.

Stardust Promises

In the cradle of night, stardust gleams,
Promises made, stitched in our dreams.
With every sparkle, a vow so true,
Stardust whispers, from me to you.

Across the void, galaxies gleam,
Holding our wishes, like a hidden theme.
In each heartbeat, the cosmos flows,
Stardust promises, wherever it goes.

Time may wane, and shadows fall,
But in this love, we've got it all.
Wrapped in magic, we'll never part,
For stardust weaves, right through the heart.

Beneath the vastness, passions ignite,
In every twinkle, we find our light.
With celestial bodies, our spirits align,
Stardust promises, eternally shine.

Awake to the truth that we both share,
A tapestry woven, forever rare.
In the harmony of the night sky's dome,
Stardust promises, guide us home.

Galactic Heartbeats

Feel the pulse where galaxies meet,
Galactic heartbeats, softly they greet.
In every thrum, a rhythm divine,
Connected in essence, your heart to mine.

Nebulas swirl in a cosmic embrace,
Each moment fleeting, we savor space.
In the silence, our spirits soar,
Galactic heartbeats, forever explore.

With every breath, the universe spins,
In this vast dance, true love begins.
Stars to witness, what fate has planned,
Galactic heartbeats, hand in hand.

Through black holes and starlit trails,
We ride the waves, as destiny sails.
In the ether where dreams reside,
Galactic heartbeats, a cherished guide.

As lightyears fade, and time won't stall,
In each heartbeat, we remember it all.
For love transcends, in the endless night,
Galactic heartbeats, our guiding light.

Radiant Connections

In the glow of dawn, new paths arise,
Radiant connections, beneath golden skies.
With every sunrise, hope takes flight,
Uniting our souls, with pure delight.

Through tangled roots, we find our way,
In vibrant colors, our spirits play.
Each heartbeat echoes, a sweet refrain,
Radiant connections, like soft summer rain.

Moments intertwined, like threads of gold,
In every glance, a story told.
With laughter shared, and tears that flow,
Radiant connections, in love we grow.

As seasons change, and time moves fast,
We'll hold forever, this bond amassed.
In every embrace, warmth will infuse,
Radiant connections, we dare not lose.

So here we stand, in a world so wide,
With hearts open wide, we'll take the ride.
For in this journey, we shine and reflect,
Radiant connections, love is perfect.

Starlit Whispers

In the quiet of the night,
Stars begin to sing so bright,
Softly weaving tales of old,
Whispers of the brave and bold.

Gentle breezes hum along,
Carrying the starlight's song,
Twinkling dreams in every eye,
Lifting hearts like clouds on high.

Beneath the velvet sky we stand,
Hand in hand, a timeless band,
Every glimmer, every spark,
Ignites our souls, ignites the dark.

Night unveils its secret dance,
Filling us with sweet romance,
Around us, constellations play,
Guiding our thoughts where wishes stray.

In the silence, close your eyes,
Feel the starlit lullabies,
In the cosmos, we reside,
Together on this mystic ride.

Cosmic Embrace

In shadows of a galaxy,
We find our cosmic symphony,
With every pulse and every beat,
The universe feels so complete.

Stars entwined in timeless grace,
We dance in a celestial space,
Gravity pulls our hearts near,
In this moment, nothing to fear.

A spiral of colors all around,
Floating softly, yet so profound,
Like stardust brushing against our skin,
A feeling deep, where love begins.

Infinite skies whisper our names,
Each twinkling light ignites the flames,
Infinite love, a comet's glow,
Together we'll travel, forever we'll flow.

In this embrace of light and dark,
We share our dreams, we leave a mark,
With cosmic kisses, hearts ablaze,
Lost in the universe's haze.

Gravitational Hearts

Two souls caught in a pull so strong,
In the dance of the cosmic throng,
With every breath, we draw near,
Gravitational love, crystal clear.

In the orbit of your gentle gaze,
Time stands still in this loving maze,
Words unspoken, yet understood,
In the silence, our hearts are good.

Nebulas wrap us in their light,
Guiding us through the velvet night,
A universe just for us,
In gravity's pull, we place our trust.

As comet trails paint the skies,
We chase the dreams that never die,
Together on this stellar quest,
Finding solace, finding rest.

So let us circle, hand in hand,
In this vast and wondrous land,
With gravitational hearts so true,
The cosmos whispers, 'I love you.'

Beneath the Moon's Caress

Beneath the moon's soft, silver light,
We whisper secrets of the night,
With stars as our watchful guide,
Together, always side by side.

The world fades into a dream,
As moonbeams dance upon the stream,
Each ripple sings the songs of yore,
With every glance, we crave more.

In this gentle, tender glow,
Love flows freely, like the river's flow,
Wrapped in twilight's warm embrace,
Finding heaven in this place.

Crickets chirp a lullaby sweet,
As time slows down, with hearts that beat,
In the silence, we find our way,
Underneath the moon's soft sway.

So let us cherish moments rare,
As moonlight weaves through tousled hair,
In every heartbeat, every sigh,
Beneath the moon, we'll always fly.

Twilight's Heartbeat

In the hush of night, whispers call,
Stars begin to waltz, shadows fall.
A gentle breeze, the trees sway slow,
Painted skies in dusky glow.

Moments linger, time stands still,
Echoes of laughter, hearts fulfill.
Moonlight dances, soft and bright,
Holding dreams throughout the night.

In this twilight, magic stirs,
Secret promises, no words occur.
Wrapped in silence, souls entwine,
Lost in love, forever shine.

Each heartbeat sings a tender tune,
Beneath the watchful gaze of the moon.
Together we weave the fabric of fate,
In the twilight, we celebrate.

Carving memories in the dark,
Every glance ignites a spark.
With each breath, our worlds align,
In this moment, love's divine.

Sunlit Affections

Golden rays caress the ground,
In warm embrace, love's found.
Laughter mingles with the breeze,
Hearts are light, like dancing leaves.

Days of warmth, laughter bright,
Moments shared in pure delight.
Hand in hand, we walk the path,
Joyful smiles, love's aftermath.

Sun-kissed mornings, we align,
Every glance feels so sublime.
Nature's beauty, love's soft glow,
In the sunshine, we both grow.

Every sunrise brings a chance,
To cherish time, to skip and dance.
With each heartbeat, bonds renew,
In the sun, our love shines through.

Fleeting moments, never fade,
In our hearts, memories made.
Together we weave the days,
In sunlit hues, love's sweet praise.

Skies of Togetherness

Beneath the vast and endless blue,
We share our dreams, just me and you.
Clouds drift slowly, a gentle sigh,
In this space, we learn to fly.

Colors merge, a palette bright,
In twilight's arms, we find our light.
Every heartbeat, echoes strong,
In the skies, we both belong.

Stars ignite, a wonderland,
With every wish, our dreams expand.
Navigating by love's refrain,
Through every storm, through every pain.

Laughter rings, like wind chimes play,
Shining moments, day by day.
With this bond, we touch the skies,
In our togetherness, love never dies.

Uniting hearts, a tapestry,
Stitched with moments, wild and free.
Underneath the vast expanse,
Together we take our chance.

Love in the Constellations

In the night, the cosmos gleams,
Whispers shared in silken dreams.
Orion watches from afar,
Guiding us, our guiding star.

Galaxies spin, timeless and wise,
In your gaze, the universe lies.
Every heartbeat draws us near,
In the silence, your voice I hear.

Mapping love in starlit skies,
Each constellation, a sweet surprise.
Stories woven through the night,
Every twinkle, pure delight.

Holding hands, we trace the lines,
Of dreams and hopes, heart entwines.
In the darkness, our love shines bright,
Guided by celestial light.

With every glance, the heavens sigh,
Two souls dancing, you and I.
In the constellations, we belong,
Together, forever, love's sweet song.

Radiant Love Under Saturn's Rings

In twilight's glow we stand so near,
Beneath the rings both bright and clear.
Our whispers dance with stardust's light,
In cosmic embrace, we feel the night.

Hearts align with the moons' soft song,
In this vast space where we belong.
The universe swirls with every sigh,
Together we reach for the endless sky.

Fragments of time spin round and round,
In the silence, our love is found.
With every pulse of the stellar beat,
We sail the skies, in love's retreat.

Through shadows cast by Saturn's glow,
In the stillness, our feelings flow.
We navigate the stars above,
In the quiet, we discover love.

Eternal glimmer in celestial hue,
Each moment shared feels ever new.
With rings of Saturn as our guide,
We dance forever, side by side.

Luminous Bonds

In the gentle light of dawn we meet,
Our hearts are woven, strong and sweet.
With every laugh, our souls entwine,
In radiant warmth, your hand in mine.

Beneath the stars, we share our dreams,
Like rivers flowing in silver streams.
Together we chase the morning's grace,
In luminous bonds, we find our place.

The world may shift, but we hold tight,
In darkest times, you are my light.
With every heartbeat, love's refrain,
We rise again through joy and pain.

Whispers of hope in twilight's breath,
In our embrace, there is no death.
The universe sings with every sound,
In shared moments, our love is found.

Through life's journey, we'll always roam,
Together, we create our home.
With tender strength, we will endure,
In luminous bonds, our hearts are pure.

Aurora of Amour

Beneath the northern lights we gaze,
In soft reflections, lovers' ways.
As colors dance across the night,
Our hearts ignite with pure delight.

Through icy winds, our voices soar,
In warmth of love, we seek for more.
Each heartbeat echoes like a song,
With you, my dear, is where I belong.

In every flicker, a promise made,
As dawn awakens, fears will fade.
With hands held close, we face the storm,
In auroras bright, our spirits warm.

In shadows deep, we find the glow,
With every step, our passions flow.
Together we cast away the night,
In this embrace, we shine so bright.

Through time and space, we'll rise anew,
In moonlit skies, it's me and you.
With every moment, love transforms,
In the aurora, our hearts are warm.

Echoes of the Night Sky

In silken darkness, dreams take flight,
Whispers linger within the night.
Stars above, like lanterns gleam,
In the stillness, we share a dream.

Time drifts softly, like a sigh,
As shadows dance, we wonder why.
In the echoes, we hear the call,
Of love that binds us, stronger than all.

With every glance, the world fades away,
In your warmth, the fears decay.
Bathed in moonlight, our spirits rise,
With boundless hope beneath the skies.

Through quiet moments, bonds grow deep,
In gentle night, our secrets keep.
Distant galaxies shimmer with grace,
As we journey to our sacred place.

In nocturnal hues, we find our way,
Through every challenge, come what may.
As echoes of the night sky blend,
In love's embrace, we transcend.

A Universe of Us

In the night sky, we dance,
Stars twinkle, a cosmic chance.
Two souls woven, a tapestry,
Infinite dreams, just you and me.

Galaxies swirl, we find our fate,
Orbits entwined, we cannot wait.
Radiant light from every heart,
Together, never to part.

Nebulas bright, colors collide,
Your hand in mine, a joyful ride.
In this vast space, we draw near,
Echoes of love, we both hear.

Together we craft, each wish and sigh,
Moments of magic, as we fly high.
Interstellar dreams, we chase the light,
In our universe, everything feels right.

Eternal echoes, soft and sweet,
Hearts beating fast, a cosmic beat.
In every corner of this grand sphere,
A universe of us, forever near.

Celestial Serenade

Moonlit whispers softly play,
Gentle breezes in our bay.
Notes of love weave through the air,
A celestial song, beyond compare.

Stars are strumming on the night,
Hope and dreams in pure delight.
Harmony in every glance,
In your eyes, I see our dance.

Galactic rhythms pulse and sway,
Melodies of night and day.
Lost in the magic of your tune,
Together we sway, beneath the moon.

Twinkling lights join our refrain,
A symphony, both joy and pain.
In this serenade, we belong,
Two hearts singing a timeless song.

Celestial bodies spin and glide,
In the universe, our love will stride.
An ethereal dance, so divine,
Forevermore, your heart is mine.

Planetary Passions

In the warmth of your embrace,
Worlds collide, a sacred space.
Fires burn on distant moons,
Our love ignited by bright tunes.

Planets spin, their orbits wide,
Feel the rush, we cannot hide.
Electric sparks spark our desires,
In this dance, our hearts conspire.

Meteor trails, a fleeting bliss,
Each moment shared, we can't dismiss.
Gravity pulls, our bodies close,
In this passion, there's no ghost.

Venus whispers secrets sweet,
In her warmth, our hearts will meet.
Mars ignites a fiery chance,
In cosmic realms, we find our dance.

As stellar tides ebb and flow,
Together, our passions will grow.
Planetary love, vast and grand,
In this universe, we take a stand.

Infinite Horizons of Love

Across the dawn, a golden hue,
Endless horizons, just me and you.
Every sunrise, a brand-new start,
Infinite paths, a shared heart.

Beyond the mountains, vast and wide,
In every journey, you're by my side.
Whispers of dreams ride the breeze,
In your embrace, I find my ease.

Rivers run deep, flowing strong,
In the current, we both belong.
The ocean kisses the sandy shore,
Infinite love, forevermore.

On horizons bright, our shadows blend,
Time may pass, but we won't end.
Together we'll face the sun's warm glow,
In every heartbeat, our love will grow.

Through twilight's dusk, we'll chase the stars,
No distance strong enough, no bars.
Infinite horizons await our flight,
With you, my love, every dream feels right.

Etherial Bonds

In whispers soft, the shadows play,
Connections formed, in light's ballet.
Invisible threads intertwine our fates,
Across the void, love resonates.

With every breath, a gentle sigh,
In silent vows, the spirits fly.
A tapestry woven, hearts aligned,
Together we wander, forever entwined.

Through distant realms, our echoes call,
In dreams we meet, beyond the thrall.
A mystical dance, in every glance,
Fate weaves its magic, a timeless chance.

Stars align, their glimmer bright,
Guiding us through the solitude of night.
Hand in hand, we'll brave the storm,
In etheric bonds, our souls stay warm.

When twilight falls, and worlds collide,
In each other's warmth, we shall abide.
An endless journey, side by side,
Etherial bonds, our hearts' true guide.

A Dance Among the Stars

Beneath the sky, where dreams ignite,
We twirl and sway in soft moonlight.
Each spark a wish, a silent song,
In this great expanse, we both belong.

Galaxies swirl, our spirits rise,
Lost in the magic of starry skies.
In cosmic rhythms, our hearts take flight,
A dance among the stars, pure delight.

With every spin, the universe bends,
As fate reveals what time transcends.
Celestial paths together we trace,
In this vast love, we find our place.

Nebulas whisper, constellations gleam,
In every glance, we share a dream.
Through scattered light, our souls entwine,
A never-ending waltz, divine.

So let the heavens guide our way,
In harmony, we'll forever stay.
A dance among the stars, a cosmic embrace,
Love ignited in endless space.

Nocturnal Affection

In shadows' grasp, we find our peace,
Where time stands still, and troubles cease.
Beneath the stars, our whispers blend,
In nocturnal embrace, hearts transcend.

Each moonlit glance, a soft caress,
In tender moments, we find our rest.
The world asleep, yet we awake,
In gentle silence, love we make.

As night unfolds, our secrets bloom,
In cozy corners, dispelling gloom.
The velvet sky, our witness true,
In this dark hour, I cherish you.

Through mystic realms, our spirits soar,
In shadows deep, we seek for more.
A lullaby sung by the stars above,
Nocturnal affection, a bond of love.

When dawn draws near, we'll fade away,
Yet in my heart, you'll always stay.
In memories bright, forever in sight,
Nocturnal affection, our shared light.

Beyond the Infinite

In realms unknown, we chase our dreams,
With every heartbeat, a new light beams.
Across the cosmos, our spirits roam,
Together we venture, far from home.

Time slips away, a fleeting guest,
In this journey, we find our rest.
Exploring depths of the great unknown,
Beyond the infinite, we have grown.

With every star, a story unfolds,
In whispered tales, our love retold.
Galactic wonders, vast and bright,
In unity's grasp, we embrace the night.

A dance of shadows, a waltz of light,
Together we shine, through endless night.
Boundless horizons, we transcend,
An odyssey of hearts, that shall not end.

Beyond the infinite, our spirits soar,
In love's embrace, we seek for more.
A journey eternal, souls entwined,
In this vast expanse, our hearts aligned.

Starlit Dreams

In the quiet of the night,
Whispers of stars take flight.
Each twinkle a secret told,
In the vastness, dreams unfold.

Moonbeams dance on silver streams,
Casting light on fragile beams.
Night's embrace, soft and warm,
A sheltering, surreal charm.

Wonders weave through velvet skies,
As dreamers soar and rise.
Caught between the dark and light,
In starlit realms, hearts unite.

Every wish a spark in the air,
A promise woven with care.
Eclipsed moments fuel the fire,
In our souls, dreams aspire.

Let us wander, hand in hand,
Through a night so grand.
With every star a guiding ray,
In starlit dreams, we'll stay.

Love Under the Aurora

Beneath the swirling skies so bright,
Our hearts ignited with pure delight.
Colors dance like flames in the night,
Holding close, it feels so right.

The aurora wraps us in its glow,
A serenade from the earth below.
Each flicker speaks of tales untold,
In every hue, our love unfolds.

Snowflakes whisper as they land,
In this moment, we understand.
With every hue, a vow we make,
In love's embrace, no hearts will break.

Through the night, our spirits soar,
Boundless dreams forevermore.
Hand in hand, we'll dance and sway,
Under the lights, come what may.

In the canvas of the night,
We'll find solace in our sight.
Love painted in celestial streams,
Forever sealed in starlit dreams.

Cosmic Tides

The moon pulls waves with gentle grace,
In this cosmic dance, we find our place.
As tides of time ebb and flow,
Secrets of the universe we know.

Galaxies swirl in a silent tune,
Under the sun, beneath the moon.
With every heartbeat, stardust sighs,
In cosmic whispers, love never dies.

A journey through the milky way,
Where dreams and reality softly play.
Each star a dream waited to be,
In the vastness, we are free.

Waves of energy flow with might,
Carrying us through the night.
In cosmic tides, we find our way,
Guided by the light of day.

Together, we drift along the stream,
Hand in hand, lost in a dream.
With every moment, forever tied,
In cosmic love, we shall abide.

Heartbeats of the Universe

In the stillness of the night sky,
Whispers of the cosmos draw nigh.
Each heartbeat echoes far and wide,
In the universe, love won't hide.

The stars sparkle like jewels on dark,
Filling our souls with a vibrant spark.
In every pulse, a symphony plays,
Melodies woven through endless days.

Galactic winds chase shadows away,
Guiding our hearts to where dreams stay.
In the gentle arms of gravity's pull,
The universe sings, forever full.

Let the stardust guide our quest,
In this infinite realm, we are blessed.
As long as the universe draws breath,
Our love will dance beyond death.

Together we weave through vast expanse,
In the rhythm of fate, we take a chance.
With every heartbeat, the cosmos spins,
In this dance of life, our love begins.

Starlit Whispers

In the night sky, secrets gleam,
Whispers of dreams, echoing beam.
Stars twinkle softly, tales unfold,
Silent stories in silver cold.

Guided by light, we wander free,
Lost in our hopes, just you and me.
Each star a memory, bright and bold,
In this vast universe, hearts we hold.

Through cosmic paths, we gently glide,
Hand in hand, across the tide.
The universe hums a soothing song,
In starlit whispers, where we belong.

Echoes of laughter, across the sky,
In every twinkle, a timeless sigh.
Night's embrace, a tender cocoon,
As we dance together, beneath the moon.

Stay with me, till dawn ignites,
Through shadows deep, and endless nights.
With each heartbeat, our spirits soar,
In starlit whispers, we seek no more.

Cosmic Embrace

In the stillness of the night,
Galaxies swirl, a wondrous sight.
Nebulae shimmer in vibrant hues,
In cosmic embrace, we find our muse.

Every heartbeat resonates true,
In the vastness, it's me and you.
Gravity pulls, our souls entwined,
In the dance of stars, love redefined.

Comets race with a fiery tail,
While constellations weave their tale.
Eternity whispers in soft caress,
In cosmic embrace, we are truly blessed.

Time stands still, as we gaze wide,
In the tapestry of space, hearts reside.
Across the void, our spirits align,
In this cosmic embrace, you are mine.

Through the universe, hand in hand,
Wanderers lost in a starlit land.
Together we'll chase the radiant light,
In this cosmic embrace, all feels right.

Love Across the Cosmos

Infinite night, where dreams ignite,
Love travels fast, a sparkling flight.
Across the cosmos, our hearts do race,
In a universe vast, we find our place.

Celestial bodies in rhythmic sway,
Though light-years apart, love finds a way.
Through nebulous clouds, we navigate,
Connected by fate, we transcend time's gate.

Stars align in a dazzling dance,
In the dark depths, we seize our chance.
Love's gravity pulls, never to part,
In the boundless sky, we share one heart.

Whispers of galaxies echo our song,
In radiant bursts, we know we belong.
As planets collide, our spirits entwine,
In the arms of the cosmos, forever divine.

Embracing the light, we soar and glide,
In the vast expanse, love is our guide.
Across the cosmos, we'll never stray,
For love is the journey, come what may.

Celestial Serenade

In twilight's glow, the stars take flight,
A celestial serenade, pure delight.
Waves of melody drift on high,
As the universe sings, 'neath the deep sky.

Planets spin in rhythm divine,
In cosmic harmony, hearts intertwine.
Each note a whisper, soft and sweet,
In this orchestral dance, we feel complete.

Galaxies twirl in a gentle embrace,
An endless ballet in expansive space.
With every pulsar's heartbeat, we feel alive,
In this celestial serenade, we thrive.

A twinkling symphony, soars above,
Each star a note, in the name of love.
Through stardust dreams, we find our way,
In this serenade of the Milky Way.

With every comet, our spirits sing,
In celestial realms, joy it brings.
As the universe breathes, so do we,
In this endless serenade, forever free.

Night Sky Whispers

Stars twinkle softly, a gentle light,
Moonbeams dance upon the night.
Whispers of dreams flow through the air,
As shadows weave their tales of care.

In silence, wishes take their flight,
Painting the canvas of the night.
Hearts awaken, secrets unfold,
In the night, stories retold.

Veils of darkness, a calming embrace,
Every twinkling star finds its place.
An orchestra of crickets sings,
To the lullaby that the night brings.

The sky, a tapestry vast and deep,
In its arms, the world softly sleeps.
Galaxies spin in a cosmic dance,
While stardust whispers of fate and chance.

In this moment, time stands still,
The heart beats gently, a tranquil thrill.
As night unfolds its mystic sighs,
We find our dreams beneath the skies.

Shadow of the Cosmos

Beneath the void, shadows creep,
In the cosmos, secrets sleep.
Nebulae swirl in vibrant hues,
Their beauty hides the ancient blues.

Planets roam in silent grace,
Drifting through this endless space.
A dark embrace, a cosmic thread,
Weaving stories of the dead.

Galaxies collide in silent bursts,
As the universe quenches its thirst.
Stars ignite, then fade away,
In the shadow's soft ballet.

Time itself a fleeting dream,
In the darkness, whispers gleam.
Each moment a flicker, a spark,
In the vast, eternal dark.

Cosmic echoes through the night,
Guide the souls seeking the light.
In the shadow of the abyss,
We find truth in a fleeting kiss.

Eclipsed Desires

In twilight's grasp, desires fade,
An eclipse where hopes are laid.
Shadows stretch across the land,
Covering dreams like shifting sand.

A silent yearning fuels the soul,
As whispers beckon to be whole.
In the dimming light, hearts confide,
The secrets buried deep inside.

Moments stolen, anguish pausing,
Light of longing swiftly dawning.
In eclipsed gaze, we find our way,
An ember's glow in shades of gray.

Tidal waves of passion rise,
Underneath the veiled skies.
Awakening sparks, tantalizing,
In shadows where desires are rising.

Yet time flows like the midnight air,
Carrying dreams beyond despair.
In the shadows, hope won't tire,
For hearts aflame will always aspire.

Celestial Dances

Starlit rhythms weave through space,
In the cosmos, a graceful trace.
Celestial bodies spin and twirl,
In the vastness, their wonders unfurl.

Planets waltz, moons softly glide,
Infinite beauty, a cosmic tide.
In the dance, a timeless embrace,
Harmony wraps the silent space.

Galactic tides pull hearts near,
In luminous circles, we cast our fear.
The universe sings a melodic tune,
Under the watchful, glowing moon.

Every spin, a tale untold,
In the night, wonders unfold.
Stars light paths where dreams take flight,
In the beauty of the night.

With each beat, the cosmos sighs,
As lovers gaze with longing eyes.
In the eternal celestial dance,
Hearts unite with fate's sweet chance.

The Stars Above Us

In the night, they softly shine,
Guiding dreams with a warm sign.
Whispers of ancient light below,
Tales of the cosmos, they bestow.

Every twinkle tells a tale,
Of lovers lost in the night pale.
Constellations dance and sway,
In the dark, they find their way.

Some wish upon a falling star,
Hoping for love, no matter how far.
Each flicker, a promise held tight,
As we gaze into the night.

Galaxies swirl in the embrace,
Creating paths in a boundless space.
The light we see, a bridge of time,
Connecting hearts in perfect rhyme.

So let us lay beneath this dome,
Where stardust weaves our cosmic home.
With every sigh and every glance,
The stars above us sing and dance.

Love in a Celestial Sea

In the abyss of a starry night,
Our hearts drift like ships in flight.
Navigating through cosmic streams,
Where love is born from shared dreams.

Waves of light, they pull us near,
With every pulse, I feel you here.
In this sea where stars align,
Your heart's rhythm beats with mine.

Celestial currents rush and flow,
Whispering secrets only we know.
In this ocean, vast and wide,
Together we sail, side by side.

Galaxies spin in a dance so bright,
Painting the heavens, igniting the night.
Each shimmer a spark, a memory clear,
In this celestial sea, our love draws near.

Through the cosmos, our souls entwine,
A love that's timeless, pure, divine.
And as we drift through starlit streams,
We'll chase forever in endless dreams.

Celestial Flares

Across the night, the flares ignite,
Colors burst, a dazzling sight.
In the sky, they weave and play,
A cosmic show that lights our way.

Each flash a spark from distant lore,
A reminder of what came before.
In this brilliance, our hearts unite,
As we bask in the firelight.

Time stands still as we behold,
The universe's stories told.
In the warm embrace of radiant hues,
We find comfort in the views.

Celestial flares will fade away,
But love remains, it's here to stay.
Through swirling trails, and bursts of light,
We dance together, hearts alight.

So let the colors fill the night,
With every flare, we feel the bright.
In a world where dreams can soar,
Celestial magic brings us more.

Moonlit Affection

Under the glow of the silver moon,
Hearts whisper soft, a gentle tune.
With every beam that lights the land,
We walk together, hand in hand.

In the hush of night, secrets unfold,
With stories of love waiting to be told.
Shadows dance in the silver light,
Guardians of dreams, holding tight.

The world fades, it's just us two,
With every glance, our feelings grew.
In moonlit whispers, we find our peace,
A timeless bond that will not cease.

Serenading stars sing melodies sweet,
As we tread softly, our hearts' heartbeat.
In the embrace of the night sky's dome,
We carve a space that feels like home.

So let the moonlight guide our way,
In this affection, we'll forever stay.
With every shadow, a promise we make,
In the heart of night, love's path we take.

Embrace of the Universe

Stars twinkle softly in the night,
Galaxies spinning, a wondrous sight.
The cosmos holds secrets untold,
In its arms, mysteries unfold.

Infinite dreams within our reach,
Lessons of love, the universe speaks.
With every heartbeat, stardust flows,
Connecting us, as time gently glows.

Planets dance in a cosmic waltz,
Each one a tale, none are at fault.
In the silence of space, we find grace,
The universe's own warm embrace.

Nebulae bloom like flowers in skies,
Painting the dark with vibrant cries.
A symphony played by celestial hands,
Echoing love through infinite lands.

In the quiet of night, together we soar,
United by dreams, always wanting more.
For in the universe, we are not alone,
In its embrace, we have found our home.

Celestial Heartstrings

In the vastness, two souls align,
Hearts entwined, like stars that shine.
Across the void, a pull so deep,
In cosmic currents, our spirits leap.

The moon whispers secrets, soft and sweet,
Guiding our paths where stardust meets.
With every pulse of the universe's heart,
We feel the magic, love's true art.

Constellations form our sacred bond,
Woven with wishes, our dreams respond.
Echoes of laughter in the solar breeze,
Filling the galaxies with joyful ease.

Time stands still in this astral embrace,
Wrapped in light, we find our place.
Through realms unknown, together we fly,
Connected forever, you and I.

As shooting stars carve paths so bright,
Each moment shared ignites the night.
In this dance of love, we'll always be,
Two hearts against infinity.

Empyrean Love Letters

Written in light, our love transcends,
Notes of affection that the cosmos sends.
Each star a word, each planet a page,
In the book of the heavens, we write our sage.

Sunbeams sketch whispers upon the night,
Each one a promise, a heart's delight.
In the silence, love's rhythm grows,
A melody only the universe knows.

Auroras dance, a vibrant decree,
Painting our story for all to see.
In the strike of comets, a kiss from afar,
Unraveling tales, no matter how far.

Every heartbeat, a stanza divine,
A symphony echoing, yours and mine.
Through time and space, we weave our fate,
An empyrean tale, love won't wait.

As celestial bodies collide and embrace,
We find our meaning in this vast space.
With each love letter written in stars,
Forever together, no matter the scars.

Whispers from Distant Worlds

Across the cosmos, subtle whispers call,
From distant worlds, where shadows fall.
In the silence, soft echoes reside,
Carrying secrets of love undenied.

Moons cradle dreams on their gentle tides,
As cosmic breezes carry our strides.
Faint flickers of light, a guiding star,
Show us the way, no matter how far.

In the dark depths of the universe's heart,
We find the stories that set us apart.
Galactic winds whisper tales of old,
In every heartbeat, a love story told.

Planets hum softly, a lullaby sweet,
In the dance of the galaxies, we find our beat.
As love travels on to the edge of night,
Each whisper a promise, a future so bright.

Through time and space, our souls interlace,
In the fabric of stars, we find our place.
For every whisper from worlds far away,
Brings us together, come what may.

The Dance of Celestial Bodies

In the night sky they twirl,
Stars ignite, a brilliant swirl.
Planets spin in graceful arcs,
Painting darkness with their sparks.

Galaxies in waltz align,
Universal steps divine.
Each rotation tells a tale,
On the cosmos, we set sail.

Comets race with shimmering tails,
Celestial whispers fill the trails.
In this vast and endless sea,
We find our place, just you and me.

Gravity pulls us ever near,
In this dance, we shed each fear.
Holding tight, we glide through space,
Embracing time in warm embrace.

As the universe expands wide,
Together, we shall not divide.
In the dance of cosmic grace,
We leave our mark, a bright trace.

Nebula of Romance

In the heart of aeons past,
Colors blend, emotions vast.
Stardust whispers in the air,
Love ignites, a cosmic flare.

Veils of gas and light combine,
Creating dreams, a grand design.
Nebulas glow, a canvas bright,
In this realm, we lose our sight.

Twinkling eyes meet in the void,
All doubts and fears are now destroyed.
Every heartbeat echoes strong,
In this place, we both belong.

From the ashes, passion blooms,
Filling endless, starlit rooms.
In every kiss, the universe,
In our hearts, love's sweet converse.

As we drift in cosmic streams,
With each glance, we weave our dreams.
In the nebula, love should stay,
Forever bound, we'll find our way.

Cosmic Connection

Across the stars, our souls collide,
In the vastness, love's our guide.
Constellations draw a map,
In this moment, we both tap.

Gravity's pull, it feels like fate,
Two lives entwined, we resonate.
Echoes of time swirl and spin,
In your arms, new worlds begin.

With every glance, the cosmos shines,
In your heart, I find my signs.
Celestial whispers in the night,
We moving forward, hearts in flight.

Link by link, our destiny knots,
In this galaxy, forget-me-nots.
Side by side, we chase the stars,
In the universe, just you and ours.

From nebulae to distant suns,
In our love, the darkness runs.
Cosmic connection, forever true,
In this expanse, I choose you.

Heartstrings in Orbit

In the silence of the space,
Our heartstrings hum with love's embrace.
Around you, I find my way,
Guided by the light of day.

Orbits cross, a dance so sweet,
In this rhythm, our hearts meet.
Every pulse, a gentle tune,
Underneath the silver moon.

With every turn, we intertwine,
Spiraling, our dreams align.
Holding tight through cosmic storms,
In your warmth, my spirit warms.

Time and space may stretch and bend,
Yet our love will never end.
As planets circle, so do we,
Bound by fate, eternally free.

In this vast galactic sea,
You and I, we're meant to be.
Heartstrings in a dance of light,
Together, we'll ignite the night.

Orbital Poetry of Love

In the dance of night skies, we twirl,
Our hearts aligned, as planets unfurl.
Through gravity's pull, our souls ignite,
Orbital whispers, love's pure light.

In this celestial embrace, we reside,
In stardust dreams, together we glide.
Each moment a verse, each glance a sigh,
As galaxies spin, we never say goodbye.

Like comets that blaze through endless dark,
We leave trails of hope, a timeless spark.
Through the cosmic vastness, our spirits soar,
A love astronomical, forevermore.

With each heartbeat echoed through the night,
Our rhythmic pulses dance with delight.
In the infinity of space, we find our way,
In the art of love, we endlessly play.

From nebulae swirling to stars on high,
Our hearts beat in tune, as we touch the sky.
In the universe's arms, we write our lore,
In the orbital poetry, we yearn for more.

Galaxies of the Heart

In the vast expanse where starlight drips,
Galaxies spin, sweet love's fingertips.
Through cosmic winds, our spirits harmonize,
Unveiling the wonder behind our eyes.

Each heartbeat a planet, each sigh a star,
Mapping our journey, no distance too far.
With every pulse, the universe sings,
Galaxies whisper, love's gentle wings.

In the dance of solar flares, we twine,
Through the dark matter, your heart and mine.
In this stellar ballet, we find our bliss,
In every embrace, a universe's kiss.

As comets trail across the velvet night,
We carve our names in infinite light.
With magnetized souls, we are forever,
In these galaxies of love, we endeavor.

Through nebulae bright where wonders start,
We weave a tapestry, galaxies of the heart.
In each tender moment, our story is spun,
As one with the cosmos, two hearts beat as one.

Stars Aligned

Under a blanket of endless night,
Stars aligned, our love takes flight.
Constellations gleam with stories untold,
In this celestial realm, we are bold.

In the depths of space, where shadows play,
Your hand in mine lights the Milky Way.
Guided by starlight, we journey afar,
In the orbits of dreams, we find who we are.

Each twinkle a memory, each pulse a song,
In the universe's arms, we both belong.
As planets embrace in a cosmic dance,
Our love's choreography, a timeless romance.

In the abyss where echoes reside,
Our hearts converge like the turning tide.
Under the glow of celestial signs,
Together forever, as the stars align.

With each breath shared beneath cosmic skies,
We echo the laughter of distant cries.
In this stellar pursuit, our souls intertwine,
In the tapestry of love, eternally shine.

Cosmic Heartbeats

In the silence between stars, we breathe,
Cosmic heartbeats, love's gentle weave.
Under supernova's glow, we unfold,
A saga of hearts, eternally bold.

With each pulse, the galaxies sway,
In this vast universe, we find our way.
Time bends and stretches, sweet dreams collide,
In these cosmic rhythms, love's faithful guide.

Through black holes and light years, we roam,
Creating our path, together, our home.
As comet tails shimmer, we soar above,
In the dance of the cosmos, we paint our love.

Each heartbeat a star, each sigh a spark,
Illuminating shadows, igniting the dark.
In this boundless expanse where moments last,
We share our secrets, entwined with the vast.

So let the universe witness our fate,
In cosmic heartbeats, our love resonates.
Through constellations bright, forever we'll glide,
In the arms of the cosmos, with love as our guide.

Beyond the Comet's Tail

In the night sky, whispers chase,
A comet's dance, a fleeting grace.
Stars align in cosmic glee,
Wishes ride on starlit sea.

Through the shadows, dreams ignite,
Guiding hearts in endless flight.
Like fireflies, they spin and swirl,
A tapestry of space unfurl.

Nebulae in vibrant glow,
Painting paths where lovers go.
In every spark, a story told,
Through the vastness, brave and bold.

With each pass, a chance we take,
To hold tight to what we make.
Moments glimmer, fade, and swell,
Beyond the comet's tail, we dwell.

As echoes fade, we look above,
In the silence, feel the love.
Guided by the stars so bright,
Forever wrapped in cosmic light.

The Gravity of Us

Pull me closer, don't let go,
Our worlds collide, a cosmic show.
In your orbit, I find my way,
Lost in this celestial play.

Each heartbeat echoes in the dark,
With every glance, ignites a spark.
You're the eclipse that steals my breath,
Between the stars, defying death.

We revolve in a dance so divine,
A universe where hearts entwine.
In the twilight, secrets spun,
Two souls merge, forever one.

The pull of you is pure and strong,
In this galaxy where we belong.
Together, we defy the night,
In the gravity of us, it feels so right.

Lean in closer, let time freeze,
In this moment, hearts at ease.
Through the cosmos, side by side,
With every step, our love, our guide.

Starry Eyed Moments

Underneath this swirling sky,
I gaze at stars and wonder why.
In their light, I see your face,
A timeless spark, a warm embrace.

Moments glitter, soft and fleeting,
Whispers of love, the heart's sweet beating.
With every twinkle, stories rise,
In the silence, truth belies.

We dance beneath the moonlit glow,
Sharing hopes only we can know.
Each sigh a comet, burning bright,
Chasing dreams into the night.

Hand in hand, we stroll in bliss,
A constellation sealed with a kiss.
In every pause, eternity waits,
As the universe celebrates.

Starry-eyed moments, pure and free,
In this vastness, just you and me.
As we drift on this cosmic wave,
In love's embrace, we'll forever crave.

Vows in the Cosmos

In the silence of the deep night,
Promising love, a vow so right.
Stars witness as we intertwine,
In this cosmic dance, we shine.

Words like stardust fill the air,
In each promise, a love affair.
Galaxies spin to hear our grace,
From here to forever, a sacred place.

Beneath the celestial parade,
The dreams we've built shall not fade.
With every heartbeat, we ignite,
An endless spark in love's pure light.

As we traverse the endless sea,
Your soul is the compass guiding me.
In the cosmos, our paths align,
For you are yours, and I am mine.

Vows in the cosmos, forever sown,
In this universe, we have grown.
Hand in hand, we face the stars,
In love's embrace, we conquer Mars.

Chasing Stardust

In the quiet of the night,
We chase the stars that gleam,
Whispers of ancient light,
A fleeting cosmic dream.

With every wish we cast,
We gather bits of fire,
A moment unsurpassed,
Fueling our desire.

Across the velvet sky,
We ride the winds of fate,
With hearts that soar so high,
To love, we navigate.

With galaxies around,
We dance in cosmic flow,
Where stardust can be found,
In every loving glow.

Together we shall roam,
Through constellations bright,
In the universe, our home,
Chasing dreams of light.

Enchanted by the Cosmos

Under an endless gaze,
We wander through the night,
Lost in a starlit maze,
Bathed in the moon's soft light.

Whispers of the unseen,
Call to our aching souls,
Echoes of what has been,
As time gently unfolds.

Galaxies spin and twirl,
Painting the skies so grand,
In this celestial swirl,
We find a place to stand.

Each twinkling gem above,
Holds secrets deep and true,
In the realm of our love,
The cosmos draws us two.

Forever intertwined,
In the stardust we roam,
Our fate, beautifully lined,
In the universe, our home.

Comet-Kissed Love

A comet streaks through night,
Its tail a blazing trail,
In the soft, pale moonlight,
Our hearts begin to sail.

With every fleeting glance,
We touch the edge of dreams,
In this cosmic dance,
Love's light forever beams.

Stars align in the dark,
Guiding our every move,
Leaving behind a spark,
In the depths, we improve.

Through the vastness we find,
Each moment, so divine,
In the silence, we're kind,
Love's comet will entwine.

Chasing our wishes high,
With passion that won't cease,
Together we will fly,
In tenacity and peace.

Constellations of the Heart

Within the stars that glow,
Our stories intertwine,
A tapestry to show,
How love can truly shine.

Charting the skies above,
With every laugh we share,
Mapping the paths of love,
With hearts forever bare.

The Milky Way we chase,
In dreams, we boldly tread,
In vastness, find our place,
Where angels fear to tread.

In constellations bright,
We find our destined roles,
Illuminated night,
Uniting our two souls.

Together, side by side,
We'll journey far and wide,
In this celestial ride,
Where forever resides.

Orbital Longing

In silence I drift, a cosmic dream,
Stars whisper secrets, the nightlight's gleam.
Gravity holds me, a painful pull,
In the vastness of space, my heart feels full.

I reach for the orbits, the twinkling light,
Each glow a promise, a wish in the night.
Beyond the horizon, where shadows play,
My spirit is tethered, in cosmic ballet.

Galaxies spiral, in beauty they twine,
The distance is vast, but your love is mine.
Forever I'm roaming, in this endless sea,
Each star a memory, a piece of thee.

The void calls softly, a lullaby sweet,
In its grand expanse, our hearts will meet.
In every rotation, I whisper your name,
My orbital longing, igniting the flame.

So let the stars guide my wandering heart,
In this universe vast, we shall never part.
Through lightyears of longing, through silence and song,
Our love is the force that keeps me strong.

Beyond the Milky Way

Past the swirling arms of our galaxy's dance,
An expanse awaits, a realm of chance.
Silent shadows linger, the cosmos so wide,
Dreams intertwining, where destinies collide.

Stars like diamonds flicker, in dark velvet skies,
Mapping the journey where eternity lies.
Time bends and sways, a mystical sway,
As we venture forth, beyond the Milky Way.

With each stellar heartbeat, I feel you near,
A cosmic connection, perfectly clear.
In the depths of nebulae, our souls will align,
Together we'll wander, through realms divine.

Galactic winds carry our whispers of love,
As we travel through stardust, below and above.
Every lightyear brings us, back to our core,
In this infinite space, I love you more.

So hold on to faith, let starlight be guide,
In the shadow of giants, let love be our stride.
Together let's leap, into the endless gray,
Beyond the Milky Way, forever we'll stay.

Ethereal Embrace

In the still of the night, where dreams take flight,
An embrace awaits, draped in moonlight.
Whispers of longing, soft as a sigh,
In this ethereal space, we learn to fly.

With eyes like the cosmos, so deep, so wide,
We dance through the stars, with hearts open wide.
Galaxies pulse in a rhythm divine,
In this moment suspended, your soul's intertwined.

Nebulae shimmer, like silk in the breeze,
Delicate trails of love, coasting with ease.
The touch of your hand, ignites the dark skies,
Filling the void, where the universe lies.

Together we wander through realms of the light,
Two halves of a whole, in the depths of the night.
With each breath of stardust, our spirits embrace,
To infinity's edge, we'll continue the chase.

So come, take my heart, let the cosmos align,
In an ethereal dream where our souls brightly shine.
Forever entwined, in this timeless space,
In love's gentle arms, we find our place.

Shooting Stars of Affection

Across the night sky, they dance and they gleam,
Shooting stars whisper, fulfilling a dream.
Each fleeting moment a tale to be told,
Of passion ignited, of love, pure and bold.

In trails of light, our wishes take flight,
Burning bright echoes of warmth in the night.
With every desire that falls from the heights,
I gather them softly, our love ignites.

The cosmos conspire to show us the way,
In the flicker of hopes, where our destinies play.
Like meteors blazing through infinite space,
In the arms of affection, we find our place.

So hold tight my heart, as the night wraps its cloak,
In this moment enchanted, let silence invoke.
Each shooting star carries a piece of our glow,
A tapestry woven, where love continues to flow.

Together we cherish these nights under skies,
Where shooting stars witness our love's sweet reprise.
In shimmering whispers, our secrets we share,
Through all of life's journeys, I know you are there.

Constellation of Desire

In the night where dreams take flight,
Stars whisper secrets, soft and bright.
Each twinkle a wish, a heart's delight,
Drawing lovers into the light.

Across the heavens, a dance unfolds,
Stories of passion, quietly told.
Hearts entwined in the cosmic mold,
A tapestry of dreams, pure gold.

Guided by moons that softly glow,
Navigating the paths we know.
In this universe of ebb and flow,
Our desires weave, radiant and slow.

With each pulse from distant stars,
Love's warmth reaches, conquering scars.
Infinite moments, no boundaries are,
In this constellation, we are ours.

So let us sail through this vast sea,
With hearts as one, just you and me.
In the universe, we'll always be,
A constellation of pure esprit.

Interstellar Yearning

Drifting through space on velvet nights,
Longing for whispers, softer delights.
In the silence, our souls take flight,
Chasing the stars, love ignites.

Every heartbeat echoes in time,
A rhythm that sings, a steady chime.
Through galaxies vast, our spirits climb,
In this dance of fate, so sublime.

Nebulae swirl, colors collide,
Our dreams intertwined, like planets glide.
In cosmic tides, we do not hide,
For love's gravity is our guide.

As comets blaze with fiery trails,
And distant worlds weave enchanting tales,
We'll wander through the cosmic gales,
In pursuit of love that never fails.

Above us, the heavens brightly yearn,
For every lesson, we must discern.
In this universe, our passions burn,
An interstellar love we'll eternally learn.

Love Across the Galaxy

From distant worlds, our hearts align,
With every pulse, our stars entwine.
Across the void, your love is mine,
A bond that stretches, pure divine.

Through cosmic winds, our whispers soar,
Echoing dreams that we adore.
In every glance, we long for more,
As galaxies watch from their shore.

In the tapestry of night, we weave,
Moments of magic, hearts to believe.
With every heartbeat, we achieve,
A love through space, we can't conceive.

Past shooting stars and Milky Ways,
I find your essence in endless rays.
Our journey paints a vibrant phrase,
For love survives through all our days.

Together through the vast unknown,
In every breath, we're never alone.
A love transcending every stone,
Across the galaxy, our hearts have grown.

Astral Emotions

In the cosmos, emotions swirl,
Like vibrant colors in a whirl.
Nebulae form as feelings unfurl,
Painting the night with a soft pearl.

Every star a dream we've made,
In this vastness, our fears cascade.
Through the darkness, hope won't fade,
With every heartbeat, love's charade.

Galactic echoes, sweet and clear,
Whispers of love only we hear.
In this vast expanse, you're always near,
An astral bond, crystal and sheer.

As planets dance in a graceful arc,
Our spirits spark, igniting the dark.
In this universe where we embark,
Love's light shines bright, a heavenly mark.

So take my hand, we'll drift away,
Through stardust dreams, forever stay.
In astral emotions, we'll play,
Creating magic in our own way.

Astral Intimacy

In the silent night, stars align,
Whispers of cosmos, you are mine.
Galaxies spin in tender embrace,
Holding you close in this timeless space.

Orbiting hearts, we dance with grace,
Gravity pulls in this endless chase.
Nebulae swirl, colors collide,
In the vastness, our dreams reside.

Celestial bodies, bright and rare,
In every glance, you're always there.
Waves of stardust, soft and bright,
Guiding our souls through the night.

Shooting stars paint stories anew,
In the dark, I find myself in you.
Cosmic rhythms echo our theme,
Together we float in this dream.

Light years apart, yet close in heart,
In this infinity, we won't part.
Astral intimacy, our sacred right,
Bound by love in the endless night.

Love's Milky Way

Through the galaxy, hand in hand,
We travel far, a journey planned.
Whispers of love amongst the stars,
Mapping the heavens, erasing scars.

In the Milky Way, hearts entwine,
Beneath the swirls, your love is mine.
Cosmic dance on this radiant beam,
Floating together, lost in a dream.

With every heartbeat, constellations glow,
Under the starlight, feelings grow.
Nebulas cradle our secrets near,
In this vast sky, I hold you dear.

Galactic winds carry our sighs,
Echoing soft in the velvety skies.
Embers of warmth in this chill expanse,
In the universe, we found our chance.

As comets blaze and planets spin,
In this vastness, our love begins.
Through space and time, let's always stay,
Together we shine in love's Milky Way.

Dreaming in Nebulas

In swirling clouds of gas and light,
We find our dreams in the tranquil night.
Colors burst in a soft, sweet sigh,
Lost in the moment as time drifts by.

Nebulas cradle our hopes and fears,
Whispers of light in celestial cheers.
Galaxies beckon with a gentle grace,
In this embrace, we share our space.

Each moment glows like a distant star,
Carried by winds, no matter how far.
In the heart of the universe, we align,
Finding our peace in the grand design.

Floating softly in cosmic dreams,
Life unfolds with its radiant beams.
Holding your hand through this grand show,
In the depth of night, our spirits grow.

As nebulas shimmer, we softly drift,
Wrapped in the magic of love's sweet gift.
Together we dream in the stardust sea,
Boundless and bright, forever free.

Harmonic Radiance

In the melody of cosmic light,
We find our harmony in the night.
Notes of starlight weave through the air,
Creating dreams, a love affair.

With every chord, your essence sings,
Carried on waves, like heavenly springs.
In the quiet hum of the endless space,
Love resonates in a timeless place.

Celestial symphony, soft and true,
In every heartbeat, I find you.
Harmonies dance in the cosmic sway,
Together we move, in love's ballet.

As planets align in perfect tune,
Stars twinkle bright, beneath the moon.
With every sunrise, our spirits rise,
Harmonic radiance, where beauty lies.

In the universe, our love's refrain,
Echoes softly like falling rain.
Forever in tune, with love's sweet sound,
In the vastness of space, we are found.

Celestial Threads

Stars glimmer in the night,
Weaving tales of worlds unknown.
Galaxies spin, a dance so bright,
Crafted in the cosmic throne.

Threads of light, they intertwine,
In the fabric of the sky.
Whispers float like aged wine,
Secrets held where dreams can fly.

Nebulas paint with vibrant hue,
Beauty in their fleeting grace.
Infinite wonders to pursue,
Each a gem in time and space.

Planets twirl in silent song,
Echoes of a timeless beat.
They remind us we belong,
In a universe so sweet.

Boundless night, a canvas wide,
Under its cloak, we find our way.
With each star, our hopes abide,
In celestial threads we sway.

Moonbeam Reveries

Beneath the moon's soft silver glow,
Dreams awaken, spirits rise.
Whispers in the night winds flow,
Bathed beneath the starlit skies.

Moonlit paths, they gently gleam,
Guiding us through shadows pale.
In this night, we dare to dream,
As dreams weave their mystic trail.

Reflections dance upon the lake,
Rippling visions come alive.
In this realm, we softly break,
Where the heart and soul can strive.

Every beam, a tale it tells,
Of lost loves and treasured grace.
Moonlit magic gently dwells,
In our thoughts, it finds its place.

As dawn approaches, dreams take flight,
Kissed by the sun's warm embrace.
Yet forever in the night,
Moonbeam reveries we trace.

Symphony of the Spheres

Planets whisper, softly sing,
In the vastness where stars abide.
A melody the cosmos brings,
Harmony in every stride.

Galactic winds tune every grace,
Celestial choirs fill the night.
Each note found in sacred space,
Resonates with pure delight.

The sun beats time with fiery heart,
While moons keep rhythm, round and round.
In this dance, we play our part,
As cosmic echoes surge and sound.

Heavenly bodies in array,
Draw us near with their embrace.
A symphony that leads the way,
In the boundless, endless chase.

Every star, a note to play,
In this opus of the divine.
In celestial night, we sway,
To the symphony that is time.

Twilight Tryst

When day meets night in soft caress,
Twilight burns with hues so rare.
Colors blend, no need to guess,
Painting skies with tender care.

A pause between the light and dark,
Whispers echo through the trees.
In this moment, we embark,
On a journey, hearts at ease.

Stars peek out from shadows deep,
Glimmers of a story untold.
In twilight's arms, we gently creep,
As secrets of the night unfold.

Every breath a sweet embrace,
Held within the dulcet air.
In this hush, we carve our space,
As romance fills the twilight's flare.

Time stands still in this delight,
Close your eyes, let dreams combine.
In the spell of fading light,
We find love in twilight's sign.

Luminous Caress

In the quiet night, stars prevail,
Whispers of light, soft as the gale.
Gentle embrace, dusk's tender kiss,
Warming our hearts, a luminous bliss.

Moonbeams dance on silver streams,
Painting our dreams, unfolding schemes.
Every glow, a promise bright,
Guiding us home through the darkest night.

Flickering hopes, flicking away,
Moments of peace at the end of day.
Each radiance sparks a new delight,
In the stillness, we find our light.

Hands entwined in softest glow,
Even in shadows, love can grow.
A gentle touch, such sweet contrast,
A luminous caress, forever cast.

Beneath the stars, we share the tale,
In the vastness, love will prevail.
Forever cherished, our hearts entwined,
In luminous dreams, we are defined.

Constellation of Hearts

In the vast expanse, we find our place,
A constellation, hearts interlace.
Each beat we share, like stars aligned,
Guiding our souls, forever entwined.

Across the night, our wishes soar,
Through the cosmos, love's ancient lore.
Every glance, a universe shared,
In quiet moments, we know we cared.

Navigating through the dark unknown,
Hand in hand, we are never alone.
With every pulse, galaxies ignite,
Creating wonders that feel so right.

In twilight's cloak, we softly speak,
Words like stardust, tender and meek.
Echoes linger, whispers of fate,
A constellation we celebrate.

Among the stars, our dreams reside,
In every heartbeat, love's gentle tide.
Through time and space, we'll drift and sway,
A constellation of hearts, come what may.

Orbiting Souls

Tracing the paths of celestial bliss,
Two orbiting souls, lost in a kiss.
In endless spirals, we dance and glide,
In the universe vast, we choose to reside.

Gravity pulls, but love lifts us high,
Through nebulae bright, we soar through the sky.
Each heartbeat echoes the rhythms of fate,
In the realm of stars, we no longer wait.

Planets align in a cosmic embrace,
Time stands still in this sacred space.
Holding our dreams in gravity's hold,
Whispers of love in the stories we've told.

Lighting the way through the dark unknown,
In orbits of trust, we have grown.
From stardust to flame, our spirits ignite,
Orbiting souls, in the heart of the night.

Together we journey, forever entwined,
The magic of love, uniquely designed.
As we whirl through the heavens, we'll find our role,
Two orbiting souls, one luminous goal.

Tidal Waves of Light

From the ocean deep, waves roll and crash,
Tidal waves of light, a brilliant flash.
Rising and falling in rhythmic grace,
Illuminating shadows, we find our place.

As the sun sets low, hues start to blend,
Colors collide, their paths will not end.
In this ocean of dreams, we drift and sway,
Riding the currents, come what may.

Beneath the surface, mysteries hide,
Tidal waves of light, we ride the tide.
Come close to the shore, let the waves embrace,
A luminescent dance, a secret space.

With each rising tide, new shores we find,
Guided by stars, our hearts aligned.
In the glow of dusk, our spirits ignite,
Tidal waves of love, so pure and bright.

So we stand together, come night or day,
In the ebb and flow, we choose to stay.
Riding the waves, through darkness and light,
In tidal waves of love, our souls take flight.

www.ingramcontent.com/pod-product-compliance
Ingram Content Group UK Ltd.
Pitfield, Milton Keynes, MK11 3LW, UK
UKHW021527280125
4335UKWH00036B/1032